Dedicated to those who value comprehensive assessment, especially upon consideration of red flags.

M.D. Tophus.

Magical Thinking Assessment Scale for Post-Traumatic Stress Disorder (MTAS-PTSD).

Hilphma Publications 2023. www.hilphmapublication.com

First Edition.

Germany.

The author has over 25 years of clinical experience in the healthcare field. Is cognisant of both DSM-5-TR (and previous versions) and ICD-11 (and previous versions) disorders and conditions; quality and safety improvement in healthcare; and healthcare education.

"Reflective Thinking: the True Healthcare Tool."
Germany: Hilphma Publications: 2022.

"Burnout in Healthcare."
Germany: Hilphma Publications: 2022.

"Reasonable Resilience in Workplaces and Healthcare Work."
Germany: Hilphma Publications: 2022.

"The Psychological Impacts of Labelling and Failure to Diagnose."
Germany: Hilphma Publications: 2022.

"The Controversy of the Remorseless and Unempathic Healthcare Worker."
Germany: Hilphma Publications: 2023.

"Attitudinal and Personality Traits in the Individual and Healthcare."
Germany: Hilphma Publications: 2023.

"Gaslighting."
Germany: Hilphma Publications: 2023.

"The Gaslighting Victims' Questionnaire (GVQ) and GVQ- Short form"
Germany: Hilphma Publications: 2023.

"Exposing Glibness in Psychopathy"
Germany: Hilphma Publications: 2023.

CONTENTS

Page

Magical thinking is common amongst Post-Traumatic Stress Disorder (PTSD), Complex Post-Traumatic Stress Disorder (Complex PTSD), and other trauma, sufferers.

The availability of assessment measures specifically tackling magical thinking and PTSD, however, is minimal.

The importance in assessing trauma related magical thinking is of high necessity as it can create: avoidance of public places (rendering the individual house bound); reduced chances of breaking out of the trauma; poor opportunities for desensitization; perturbation/constant trauma related ideation becoming a minute to minute focus; being consumed by victim identity; further withdrawal from reality, people, or recognising need for support, interaction and, help; risk of developing other clinical disorders; increased negative thinking; higher anxiety; entrenchment of compulsive thoughts and behaviors; and, higher risk of self-harm.
These are just some of the consequences of magical thinking in PTSD/Complex PTSD/trauma. Identification and diagnosis of such, therefore, becomes essential.

The Magical Thinking Assessment Scale for PTSD (MTAS-PTSD) includes areas of assessment, such as: dissociation; avoidance; negative changes to thoughts and emotions; depersonalization; significant changes to physiological reactivity; intrusive cognitions; and, derealization.

Specifically, consideration of the following was undertaken to assist in developing the MTAS-PTSD measure:

-constantly repeated phrases

-ritualistic actions

-planned, strategic actions (to prevent bad outcomes)

-thought action fusion (concept of being morally corrupted because of thought about an action but sans undertaking actual action)

-exaggerated expectations of danger

-underestimation of coping skills

-poor threat estimation

-catastrophic thinking

-over-responsibility

-perfectionism

-control.

It was derived from identified trauma themes and thence, categorised:

1/ irrational thought; panic; intrusive thoughts; hypervigilance, hyperalert mood.

2/ indirect triggers (time of day, word references on shop windows, unrelated discussions by others, loudness of noise, people walking behind or directly toward/bumping into/close proximity/invasions of personal space).

3/ no explanation nor reason for being the victim (bad luck, wrong place at wrong time, wrongly targetted, random attack).

4/ protective measures (expecting the unexpected, everyone is perceived as a danger, not left alone to grieve the trauma suffered); obsessive-compulsive tendencies (including checking behaviors and, contamination concerns); loss of control, uncontrollable environments; obedience or hostile based thinking as a form of control and prevention of further incidences.

5/ regressive thoughts and behaviors; perceived externalisation of private thoughts to affect objects and things.

6/ cultural, spiritual beliefs- ultimately its the reliance on use as a form of protection or other in PTSD/Complex PTSD/ other trauma disorders is at issue (return to roots, advisors/support people are reinforcing such); one is drawn to certain beliefs because it fits the magical thinking internal narrative, for instance).

7/ thought projection.

8/ past experience of criticism by others; hypersensitivity.

9/ overestimation of threat; fear factor; catastrophising; panic attacks (and fear of); expectations that one will always be abused in some way, is destined for it.

10/ intolerance of uncertainty (loss of control); unpredictability (not handled well); learned helplessness.

11/ not trusting PTSD/Complex PTSD/other trauma related disorders' symptomatology and how it can turn (being done to versus working with); PTSD/Complex PTSD/ other trauma- concept that all is internalised (internal locus of control); thought suppression breaks in public arena and elsewhere (which leads to culmination toward elevated trauma symptoms after the fact).

12/ ineffective cognitive regulation strategies; reductions in effective cognitive processing; misinterpretation of micro-gestures- processing anomalies/misperceptions.

13/ trauma related adrenalin rush; physical factors: high cortisol activation.

14/ unconscious self-punishment; shame; worry; rumination; self-blame.

15/ concept of increased responsibility (dovetails with self-blame) compared with others; perfectionistic overtones.

16/ reduced self-efficacy; problems with self-reliance; not trusting self; self-doubt about coping mechanisms.

17/ complex rules for intimates, self, society; detachment or estrangement from other individuals; aloneness- everyone becomes the enemy due to perceived lack of compassion, or lack of support.

18/ constant expectations that one is a target/vulnerable/a perpetual victim; imagined threat; persistent, exaggerated negative beliefs; distorted beliefs; confusion.

The M.D. Tophus' Magical Thinking Assessment Scale for Post-Traumatic Stress Disorder (MTAS-PTSD) incorporates 2 sections: a brief structured interview (section 1); and a 50-item rating scale (section 2). The 50-item rating scale has 3 subscales: Indirect; Direct; and, Induced, magical thinking. The MTAS-PTSD comprehensively assesses magical thinking in Post-Traumatic Stress Disorder, Complex Post-Traumatic Stress Disorder, and other related Trauma disorders. Guidelines and recommendations are included to assist the assessor.

MTAS-PTSD basic details:

The MTAS-PTSD clinician administered measurement involves a:

-brief structured interview (section 1); and

-a 50-item rating scale (section 2)

which assesses the existence, and level, of magical thinking in Post-Traumatic Stress Disorder/Complex Post-Traumatic Stress Disorder/related Trauma based disorder sufferers.

The 50-item rating scale has 3 Magical Thinking subscales: Indirect; Direct; and, Induced.

It has been specifically created to cater for the gap in psychological measures regarding magical thinking and its interrelationship with traumatic stress disorders' symptomatology.

Assessor eligibility:

Both the interview section (section 1) and the rating scale (section 2) of the MTAS-PTSD are to be administered by clinicians with knowledge, skills, and training, in dealing with PTSD (and/or Complex PTSD), and other trauma related, clients and assessees.

Respondent/ Client age range:

The MTAS-PTSD is suitable for persons aged 16 years and over.

Respondent/Client focus:

Ideally, prior to administering the MTAS-PTSD assessment, the respondent must have received a diagnosis of PTSD or Complex PTSD or a related trauma based disorder.
The assessment scale can also be used for those individuals who are in the process of having their trauma symptoms diagnosed.

The focus of the MTAS-PTSD measure is not to provide assistance in diagnosing, for example, schizotypal personality disorder, or alternative explanations for the existence of magical thinking symptomatology.

If the administering (or related) clinician suspects that there is indeed an adjunctive, or alternative, diagnosis to PTSD/Complex PTSD/trauma based magical thinking, then the onus is upon them to seek out additional relevant assessment measurements.

Process of administering the MTAS-PTSD:

Upon introducing the administration of the MTAS-PTSD, the assessor is to give a brief description of magical thinking to the respondent, without providing extensive examples of such.

For instance, one could say *'magical thinking involves believing that your thoughts and/or rituals and/or desires can directly cause certain behaviors or circumstances in other individuals, groups, or society'.*

Clarification of key abbreviations:

Post-Traumatic Stress Disorder is referred to as PTSD.

Complex Post-Traumatic Stress Disorder is indicated by Complex PTSD.

Extraneous respondent/client variables for consideration:

In relation to extraneous variables, there is the issue of a respondent's traumatic memory loss, detachment, or dissociative issues.

These can affect memory and cause memory deficit (either temporary, or otherwise).

Client disclosure of previously diagnosed conditions, along with the assessor's observation skills and professional intuition, may elicit this as a consideration.

Some questions are included specifically to ensure consistency, and reliability, of responses provided.

(This is synonymous with the M.D. Tophus 'Gaslighting Victims' Questionnaire', and 'Gaslighting Victims' Questionnaire- Short form'.)

Additional recommended assessment/s:

Clinician inspired, dependant upon clinical decision-making, knowledge, skill, expertise, and may involve referral to an alternative service to satisfy specific additional assessment requirements.

MTAS-PTSD and recognising risk:

Please see below for more regarding assessment of risk (that is, yellow and red flag alerts).

Scoring and results:

Please see page 42. Each subscale is summed, and then the 3 subscales summed for the total score.
Score parameters are provided, accordingly.

It is absolutely advisable for the assessor to ask for clarification from the respondent about any
highly rated responses which correspond with yellow and red flag alerts (as featured on the next page).
An asterisk is provided (in the scale- section 2) against each of the flags' based statements, for the assessors convenience.

'Yellow flags' are considered moderate to high alerts for risks to safety, or need for clarification of risk to safety.

'Red flags' are considered high to very high alerts for risks to safety, or need for clarification of risk to safety.

	RED FLAGS
(item 3) Asking for help puts me in danger	(item 7) I must guard myself from imminent danger
(item 19) I can predict when bad things are about to occur	(item 8) Everyone is a danger to me
(item 37) I deserve to be punished	(item 25) If I think about hurting myself then it will come true
(item 47) I do not have the ability to cope	(item 26) If I think about hurting others then it will come true

ASSESSMENT:
MAGICAL THINKING ASSESSMENT SCALE IN PTSD (MTAS-PTSD)

NAME of CLIENT/RESPONDENT	
CLIENT'S/RESPONDENT'S DATE of BIRTH	
DATE ADMINISTERED	
NAME of ASSESSOR	
ASSESSOR'S RECOMMENDATIONS for further ASSESSMENT MEASURES and/or IMMEDIATE INTERVENTIONS	

Basic Instructions:

Both the interview section (section 1) and the rating scale (section 2) of the MTAS-PTSD are to be administered by clinicians with knowledge, skills, and training, in dealing with PTSD (and/or Complex PTSD), and other trauma related, clients and assessees.

The MTAS-PTSD is suitable for persons aged 16 years and over.

Please observe yellow and red flag alerts' recommendations, and ask for clarification from the respondent following administration of Section 2.

It is essential to provide the assessee with a visual representation of the response scoring (1 to 5) prior to administering of section 2 to ensure accuracy of responses given.

Upon introducing the administration of the MTAS-PTSD, the assessor is to give a brief description of magical thinking to the respondent, without providing extensive examples of such.

For instance, one could say *'magical thinking involves believing that your thoughts and/or rituals and/or desires can directly cause certain behaviors or circumstances in other individuals, groups, or society'.*

Initial questions to be administered before the MTAS-PTSD rating scale section:

1/ Have you been diagnosed with PTSD or Complex PTSD or another trauma related disorder?

2/ If so, when were you diagnosed?

3/ If so, who provided the diagnosis?

4/ Have you received treatment for PTSD/Complex PTSD and/or any other type of trauma related disorder?
Please provide details (recency, length, by whom, where, type of treatment).

5/ What is the reason for undertaking the MTAS-PTSD assessment?

6/ Which kind of supports do you have for your clinical issues?
   (frequency, planned post-assessment, current referral options).

7/ Do you have access to emergency support?
 (If not, clinician to provide emergency counselling or other 24-hour phone contact details of an agency, etc).

8/ Explain that the clinician/related other administering the scale may need to access immediate support options on behalf of the respondent in the event of yellow or red flags' alerts which may arise during the assessment scale results' process.

INDIRECT Subscale:

1/ I avoid thinking about negative incidents to stop them from happening

1	2	3	4	5
Never	Rarely	Sometimes	Often	Always

2/ Wishing as a ritual is important to me

1	2	3	4	5
Never	Rarely	Sometimes	Often	Always

* 3/ Asking for help puts me in danger

1	2	3	4	5
Never	Rarely	Sometimes	Often	Always

4/ Because I have become a victim I am in tune with the supernatural

1	2	3	4	5
Never	Rarely	Sometimes	Often	Always

5/ Being assertive causes bad events to occur

1	2	3	4	5
Never	Rarely	Sometimes	Often	Always

6/ People stare at me when I go out

1	2	3	4	5
Never	Rarely	Sometimes	Often	Always

* 7/ I must guard myself from imminent danger

1	2	3	4	5
Never	Rarely	Sometimes	Often	Always

* 8/ Everyone is a danger to me

1	2	3	4	5
Never	Rarely	Sometimes	Often	Always

9/ I am concerned that I will verbalise my inner voice to others

1	2	3	4	5
Never	Rarely	Sometimes	Often	Always

10/ If something really negative does not happen to me everyday then I know something catastrophic will soon occur

1	2	3	4	5
Never	Rarely	Sometimes	Often	Always

11/ People make gestures toward me which means that I am about to be victimised again

1	2	3	4	5
Never	Rarely	Sometimes	Often	Always

INDIRECT Subscale Summed Score:----------------------(mean=----------)

<u>**DIRECT Subscale:**</u>

12/ I wear a certain colour so that nothing bad will happen to me

1	2	3	4	5
Never	Rarely	Sometimes	Often	Always

13/ I say specific words multiple times per day to ensure my safety

1	2	3	4	5
Never	Rarely	Sometimes	Often	Always

14/ If I get a red traffic light (when driving) I know that I will have a bad day

1	2	3	4	5
Never	Rarely	Sometimes	Often	Always

1	2	3	4	5
Never	Rarely	Sometimes	Often	Always

1	2	3	4	5
Never	Rarely	Sometimes	Often	Always

1	2	3	4	5
Never	Rarely	Sometimes	Often	Always

18/ I must greet and farewell every time that I see someone so that nothing bad happens to them

1	2	3	4	5
Never	Rarely	Sometimes	Often	Always

* 19/ I can predict when bad events are about to occur

1	2	3	4	5
Never	Rarely	Sometimes	Often	Always

20/ I avoid certain numbers

1	2	3	4	5
Never	Rarely	Sometimes	Often	Always

| 21/ Holding my breath to ward off danger is effective |

| 1 | 2 | 3 | 4 | 5 |
| Never | Rarely | Sometimes | Often | Always |

| 22/ I talk to objects in my house to make sure that they keep functioning |

| 1 | 2 | 3 | 4 | 5 |
| Never | Rarely | Sometimes | Often | Always |

| 23/ Fighting with others can jinx me or the other person |

| 1 | 2 | 3 | 4 | 5 |
| Never | Rarely | Sometimes | Often | Always |

24/ If I avoid praying then I will be punished by god/higher power

1	2	3	4	5
Never	Rarely	Sometimes	Often	Always

*** 25/ If I think about hurting myself then it will come true**

1	2	3	4	5
Never	Rarely	Sometimes	Often	Always

*** 26/ If I think about hurting others then it will come true**

1	2	3	4	5
Never	Rarely	Sometimes	Often	Always

| 27/ Taking hold of certain objects makes bad things happen |

1	2	3	4	5
Never	Rarely	Sometimes	Often	Always

| 28/ I blink and/or touch things a certain number of times so that I am safe |

1	2	3	4	5
Never	Rarely	Sometimes	Often	Always

| 29/ When I go out amongst strangers I believe that they know about the traumatic incident which I have suffered |

1	2	3	4	5
Never	Rarely	Sometimes	Often	Always

30/ People talk in code, or in circles, around me. This means that I am guilty of something.

1	2	3	4	5
Never	Rarely	Sometimes	Often	Always

31/ If my pulse rate is high then I immediately fear that I will die

1	2	3	4	5
Never	Rarely	Sometimes	Often	Always

DIRECT Subscale Summed Score: --------------(mean=--------)

<u>**INDUCED Subscale:**</u>

32/ I become distressed when I try to think of ways in which I can control situations

1	2	3	4	5
Never	Rarely	Sometimes	Often	Always

33/ I have problems differentiating between fantasy and reality

1	2	3	4	5
Never	Rarely	Sometimes	Often	Always

34/ I believe that I have psychic abilities

1	2	3	4	5
Never	Rarely	Sometimes	Often	Always

35/ I avoid being assertive with other people

1	2	3	4	5
Never	Rarely	Sometimes	Often	Always

36/ I feel guilty about everything

1	2	3	4	5
Never	Rarely	Sometimes	Often	Always

* 37/ I deserve to be punished

1	2	3	4	5
Never	Rarely	Sometimes	Often	Always

38/ Being positive when you are traumatised is for fools				
1	**2**	**3**	**4**	**5**
Never	Rarely	Sometimes	Often	Always

39/ I worry about everything				
1	**2**	**3**	**4**	**5**
Never	Rarely	Sometimes	Often	Always

40/ I plan ahead to prevent every possible negative outcome				
1	**2**	**3**	**4**	**5**
Never	Rarely	Sometimes	Often	Always

41/ I analyse events for hours				
1	2	3	4	5
Never	Rarely	Sometimes	Often	Always

42/ I reinterpret conversations for hours				
1	2	3	4	5
Never	Rarely	Sometimes	Often	Always

43/ I cannot control thinking about bad things which have happened to me				
1	2	3	4	5
Never	Rarely	Sometimes	Often	Always

44/ I think about bad things which have happened to me all day

1	2	3	4	5
Never	Rarely	Sometimes	Often	Always

45/ I trust noone

1	2	3	4	5
Never	Rarely	Sometimes	Often	Always

46/ I do not trust myself

1	2	3	4	5
Never	Rarely	Sometimes	Often	Always

*** 47/ I do not have the ability to cope**				

1	2	3	4	5
Never	Rarely	Sometimes	Often	Always

48/ I am scared that I will have a panic attack in front of others				

1	2	3	4	5
Never	Rarely	Sometimes	Often	Always

49/ I worry about my trauma triggers being seen by other people				

1	2	3	4	5
Never	Rarely	Sometimes	Often	Always

<table><tr><td>50/ I am hyperalert</td></tr></table>

1	2	3	4	5
Never	Rarely	Sometimes	Often	Always

INDUCED Subscale Summed Score:------------------(mean=--------)

TOTAL SCORE (Summed Subscale Scores)-----------(mean=---------)

RED FLAGS:...

YELLOW FLAGS:...

INTERVENTION/S (IMMEDIATE/OTHER):...

To ascertain the mean score, please sum the scores and divide by the number of items (so too, with the subscales).

Score Ranges:

<u>TOTAL scores (total number of items: 50):</u>

minimum: 50-122
moderate: 123-173
high: 174-250.

<u>Subscale INDIRECT magical thinking (11 items):</u>

minimum: 11-29
moderate: 30-40
high: 41-55.

<u>Subscale: DIRECT magical thinking (20 items):</u>

minimum: 20-45
moderate: 46-65
high: 66-100.

<u>**Subscale INDUCED magical thinking (19 items):**</u>

minimum: 19-48
moderate: 49-73
high: 74-95.

Naturally, even in the instance of a high magical thinking score being consistent with PTSD/Complex PTSD/ related trauma based disorders only, then further interventions to alleviate the assessee's suffering must be put in place.

Especially if the respondent indicates perturbation of harm to self, or others. Then the assessor must investigate, intervene and report, in line with ethical standards and/or mandatory reporting requirements.

Furthermore, immediate recognition and response regarding risk and danger to person, heeding of police/ legal official warnings of danger in public places (especially, specific to the individual respondent), and existence of witness protection circumstances, is necessary.

Other individuals' gossip about the respondent, such as: traumatic incident disclosure, past trauma history disclosure, discussion of media coverage (for high profile incidents), witnessing of the event then news spread among locals, naming of the exact location where the trauma took place, may all influence the magical thinking and other related PTSD/Complex PTSD and trauma related symptomatology, and certainly the MTAS-PTSD scale results.

The effects of cultural, or spiritual, beliefs must be taken into account. However, the focus of the assessment is upon magical thinking as impact/symptomatology related to PTSD or Complex PTSD and trauma and thus, requires this direct thematic concentration.

9 798885 775668 3